On Your Bike!

Tom was on his old bike.
He was going fast.
He was going too fast.

Tom did not see the big hole. He went into it.

PEDAL POWER

Contents

Jeremy Taylor

Story illustrated by
Steve May

Before Reading

In this story

 Tom

Tricky words

- hole
- hedge
- field
- nettles
- haystack
- pitchfork
- pool

Introduce these tricky words and help the reader when they come across them later!

Story starter

Tom likes all kinds of sport. One day, he went off on his bike, but he went too fast. He did not see a big hole in the road. He flew off his bike towards a hedge.

The bike fell over.
Tom flew over the hole.
He was going into a hedge.

"Aaargh!" said Tom.

But Tom was lucky.
He did not go into the hedge.
He flew over it. But ...

... in the field were some nettles. Tom was going into the nettles.

"Aaargh!" said Tom.

Why is Tom worried about the nettles?

7

But Tom was lucky.
He did not go into the nettles.
He was going into a haystack.

But ...
in the haystack was a pitchfork.

"Aaargh!" said Tom.

But Tom was lucky.
He did not go into the haystack.
He flew over it.

But Tom was not so lucky.
In the field was a pool of mud.

"Aaargh!" said Tom.

Will Tom land
in the mud?

Tom fell into the mud.
"Yuk!" he said.

Quiz

Text Detective

- Why did Tom fall off his bike?
- Do you think Tom was lucky?

Word Detective

- **Phonic Focus:** Blending three phonemes

  Page 4: Can you sound out 'did'?
- Page 3: Find a word that means 'quickly'.
- Page 8: Find a word made from two words.

Super Speller

Read these words:

going   too   went

Now try to spell them!

HA! **HA! HA!**

Q How does a snowman get to work?

A By icicle!

13

Before Reading

Find out about

- The different kinds of bikes people ride

Tricky words

- racing
- dangerous
- mountain
- crazy
- world
- France

Introduce these tricky words and help the reader when they come across them later!

Text starter

Bike riding is great fun. Some people like mountain bike racing and some people race around France. Other people like doing stunts. You can even ride a bike with one wheel!

All Kinds of Bikes

Some people like to do BMX bike racing.

It looks great fun.
But it can be dangerous
so they always wear a helmet.

Some people like to do mountain bike racing.

It looks great fun but it can be muddy.

Some people like to do
speed bike racing.
They wear crazy helmets.

Some people like racing bikes around France.

It's the world's biggest bike race, but it can be dangerous.

Why do you think this is a dangerous race?

Some people like riding
bikes around the world.
They must be crazy!

Some people like to do stunt bike riding.

It can be dangerous, so they wear helmets too. It looks great fun!

Some people like riding a bike with one wheel.

They must be crazy!

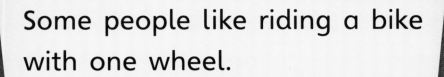

Do you know what this bike is called?

Do you like riding a bike?

Riding bikes can be great fun, but always wear a helmet.

Quiz

Text Detective

- Why is wearing a helmet a good idea?
- What sort of bike would you like to ride?

Word Detective

- **Phonic Focus:** Blending three phonemes
  Page 17: Can you sound out 'fun'?
- Page 19: Find a three-syllable word.
- Page 23: Which sentence is a question?

Super Speller

Read these words:

must   be   they

Now try to spell them!

HA! HA! HA!

 Why did the turkey pop a wheelie?

To prove he wasn't chicken.